Management and Leadership

Management and Leadership

IMPROVING PERFORMANCE
IN TIMES OF CRISIS.
A PRACTICAL GUIDE.

Stavros Baroutas

Copyright © 2011 by Stavros Baroutas.

Library of Congress Control Number: 2011962850
ISBN: Hardcover   978-1-4691-3873-2
               Softcover   978-1-4691-3872-5
               Ebook   978-1-4691-3874-9

All rights reserved. No part of this book may be reproduced or transmitted in any form or by any means, electronic or mechanical, including photocopying, recording, or by any information storage and retrieval system, without permission in writing from the copyright owner.

This book was printed in the United States of America.

Contact author: *info@baroutas.com* or *www.baroutas.com*
Contact translator: *mampelourgou@yahoo.com*

To order additional copies of this book, contact:
Xlibris Corporation
0-800-644-6988
www.XlibrisPublishing.co.uk
Orders@XlibrisPublishing.co.uk

Contents

Introduction 7

PART I

1.1 Personal Development 13
1.2 Steps to Personal Improvement 17
1.3 Get Creative 21
1.4 Perception 28
1.5 Personal Benchmarking 33
1.6 Improving one's attitude 41

PART II

2.1 Management in Times of Crisis 49
2.2 Training 53
2.3 Heroes; the leaders of tomorrow 58
2.4 Management 63
2.5 The leader; you 65

Conclusion 69
Bibliography—Sources—Ideas 73

Introduction

How often do you flirt with the thought of writing a book?

Writing is a path to creation, through constant development and reorganisation of material, eventually leading in a far richer outcome than when relying merely to thought. After all, language was not devised for the purpose of enhancing introspection. Therefore, written speech is often a most suitable means for such a scheme.

This book aims at introducing several ideas and theories related to self-motivation and improvement, in both a professional and a personal level. It does not aspire to take the reader to the moon and back, but, as someone once phrased it, "if it is a book, then it must be worth something." In effect, the book encompasses a combination of management and psychology theories and concepts, which aim at constructing a wider perception of external reality, at the same time stimulating a better attitude towards other individuals. All these incorporated in one sole objective.

It further aims to develop the competitiveness of all of us who live in today's 'jungle', in order to contribute to the construction of a better society. Indeed, no claim is made as to holding the absolute recipe for success of such an ambitious scheme. Nevertheless the book constitutes an attempt towards this direction; an observation of the self-interest which pervades today's societies. As Marcus Aurelius suggested, "a man's worth is no greater than the worth of his ambitions." [Meditations, 7.3, c. 170]. Very few things tend to be as frustrating as failing to meet one's objectives, despite genuine will to struggle.

Individuals should be well-disposed to change without failing to consider high values and virtues. After all, change is the very essence of life; an equation of development and wear. Hence, change of attitude towards the society and the companies—constituting models of society themselves—as well as constant manipulation we currently suffer has led us to the point of suffocation. We have become, thus, reluctant to accept what is 'passed on' to us on a daily basis and we refuse to submit to enslavement. Instead, we opt for a different kind of chains; the ones constructed when people join hands and unite for the sake of creation.

Creativity is individuals' capacity to visualise numerous abstract concepts which enable them to figure new ideas, alternative methods and new modes of rendering their schemes more effective. It is the driving force to change as individuals and learn how to form genuine relationships with other people. After all, this is what communication is all about; relationships. The purpose of messages involved in such a form of communication is achieving a higher rate of satisfaction out of everyday acquaintances; in other words, circumstances and interpersonal relationships which fill us with joy and a sense of completeness and reward. Concepts and ideas in the book should be read in conjunction to each other, under a cautious, critical eye.

Ignorance is an unfortunate principle which impedes self-development and progress.

On the basis of the above-mentioned parameters, the book is divided in two parts. The first part mirrors the author's attempt to point out strategies related to personal and collective perception of improvement, as well as to criticise established rigid attitudes. In the second part, a new profile of leadership is delineated by means of current management principles, along with the way in which management responds to current crisis.

PART I

1.1

PERSONAL DEVELOPMENT

> *One's ultimate life-purpose is "individual journeys toward his or her own individual peaks of spiritual growth."*
> *Scott Peck (1978).*

Personal development is about being on alert; never getting bored. According to theories of chaos management, individuals should be restless and competitive in order not to cease to progress. Nowadays, foresight of forthcoming events tends to be less important than the actual nature of reaction to given circumstances.

Stress is not an issue when it comes to references of individuals' psychosomatic state in the book. It is the case of development and improvement, irrespective of stress. Individuals should release themselves from stress and attempt to think more clearly.

At this point, one might wonder what personal development is in the first place and what reasons dictate it. The answer is multifold. Personal development is what aids individuals acquire a sense of purpose in life. Moreover, it enables self-improvement, both in a professional and in a personal level. Along the same lines, personal development engages individuals to everyday action, rendering them active citizens of autonomous will. In the long turn, only time will prove what they will have actually achieved.

Likewise, personal development is about feeling alive, learning from previous personal or other people's experiences, planning the future and the next steps towards the realisation of certain goals. It is also about being insightful, reading, listening, seeing and observing at the same time. Such aspirations often require making constant effort and exceeding one's own limits. In any case, individuals should be consistent as to their words and actions.

Accordingly, personal development entails questioning everyday reality. Critical thinking is crucial at this point. Individuals should develop judgment, in order to be able to interpret different phenomena and circumstances. After all, the brain is like a muscle; lack of exercise leads to atrophy.

Personal development unfolds in two levels. The first is the one called technocratic or social. At this level, individuals attempt to ascend the hierarchy ladder or—in case they do not manage or are not allowed to do so—they merely work in order to survive. The second level is the personal one. It is the least regarded in today's society and the place for improvement of individuals' inner world. We should all try to hold control over our capabilities, have an unbiased view of our own, as well as self-control and a sober judgment.

Investing in this personal level enables us to focus on our inner self and our families. We also learn how to be more flexible and respond effectively to various difficulties occurring in everyday life.

There is a quote saying that "the mind is not a vessel to be filled but a fire to be kindled." Nevertheless, no fire can be kindled by this cascade of orders, factitious needs and desires each individual is subject to nowadays, neither by advertisements to be digested without critical thinking. Instead, human values, along with independent thinking, must be cultivated, thereby leading in a change of attitude which shapes the personality of a leader; one who minds his or her own attitude and at the same time affects other individuals' conduct.

This is a stage of personal inner development. It is self-improvement for the sake of our own self. Improving one's values entails a change in attitude which is bound to prove positive for both personal and professional affairs. The starting point for change must be our own self. Only after changing ourselves is it possible to impart knowledge and proper modes of conduct to other individuals, shaping proper characters according to suitable patterns of behaviour.

In past, more innocent times when we were younger, our thoughts knew no boundaries. We were proud and modest at the same time. We had a thirst for knowledge. We had every virtue an individual would need to hold. Whenever we set our mind onto something, we would do everything in our power to achieve our goal. Alas; once we got older, such attributes disappeared. We lost our imagination and sense of humour. Instead, we have become serious and stern. We have lost our spontaneity, creativity and our ability to associate concepts with pictures.

Naturally, self-judgement and judgement of other individuals requires the establishment of certain steps to be followed. Likewise, specific criteria are necessary for achieving personal improvement.

According to E. P. Papanoutsos, a proper citizen should essentially be a free individual; and a free individual is one who claims freedom every single moment in life. Personal freedom is only achieved after intense inner struggle. It is in the inner self where heroism and courage lie, which are necessary to release oneself from ignorance, prejudice, delusions and whatever impedes growth and self-realisation. "Only a free individual can be morally autonomous." In other words, individuals who aspire to improve in a personal or professional level must try and release themselves from inner delusions, demystifying people and situations. Therefore, you should try to release yourselves from feelings of awe for certain people or circumstances. Consider whether they would be any different in case they did not acquire the position they currently hold and reconsider your attitude towards them.

Likewise, you should demystify your surrounding circumstances, whether they are of social or consumerist nature. Try to release yourselves from prejudice. The issue of prejudice is addressed in almost every communication seminar. If only prejudice is not eliminated, proper communication between individuals and wider social groups is impossible. An analogy could be drawn here with the case of two people engaged in a conversation, one of whom disapproves of the other one's outfit. This discrepancy in taste often leads in distraction and disapproving stares which impede the harmonious flow of conversation between the two interlocutors. This should not be the case. Simplicity is among the virtues to be pursued by all individuals. We should learn to treat other people as individuals with whom we share the same essential needs, hopes and concerns.

In this respect, it is useful to read the stories of successful individuals and attempt to follow their steps. Likewise, it is of much importance to read books and articles promoting creative thinking, particularly those that have to do with creative writing. The process of devising an innovative concept constitutes a huge step and requires putting things under an entirely new perspective. It also calls for knowledge, intuition and creativity.

Finally, it is advisable to attend seminars, conversations and workshops and do whatever might prove to be a source of inspiration for further steps. New experiences are a gateway to the breeding of a new mode of life.

1.2

STEPS TO PERSONAL IMPROVEMENT

> *"Penetrating so many secrets, we cease to believe in the unknowable. But there it sits nevertheless, calmly licking its chops"*
>
> H. L. MENCKEN

6. Judge

5. Synthesise

4. Identify essential individual elements

3. Use

2. Comprehend

1. Remember

The above, according to Socrates, constitute unconscious mental processes which underlie every thinking attempt. At this point, reference will be made to the primary stages involved in any thinking process, rather than to the various categories of memory or the timespan of memory retention.

Steps between the second and the sixth stage put individuals' synthesising capacity into question. Most of us often fail to pay the proper amount of attention to what lies around us. We tend not to observe or critically think about external reality. The reason for such an attitude may lie in the multiplicity of our experiences, as well as in the images, combinations and syntheses involved in any thinking process. Individuals who aspire to progress, improve their capacities and perceive of difference should be open-minded and should develop synthesising skills, in much the same way as Albert Einstein made his way to creation through different, seemingly unrelated fields. The last one is not a path of reason. Reason often acts as a confinement to the extent of variance which underlies individuals' actions. Therefore, the primary emphasis should be laid on creative thinking, which often helps us think different, unlike the meticulous analysis dictated by reason. Thinking processes are not meant to be constrained in narrow limits.

The concept of humour is closely associated with alternative thinking processes. A humourous approach allows the mind to waver between predictable ways of perceiving reality and others, less predictable and yet equally possible.

An essential principle in any alternative thinking process is realising that a dominant idea might as well be the source of trouble, instead of being beneficial. Therefore, you should avoid being obsessed with dominant ideas but rather attempt to isolate them. Through determining and recording such ideas it is possible to avoid their polarising effect. Their analysis must be cautious and conscientious.

It is often argued that no one has the right to question another individual's view, unless a plausible alternative can be suggested. Nevertheless, such a rationale might as well constitute an effective means of inhibiting the creation of new ideas. How can it be possible to develop new modes of synthesising concepts and at the same time keep the old ones intact? Seeking for new ideas in the framework of old theories is merely a waste of time. Likewise, comparison between new and old modes of synthesising concepts lacks essential meaning. In this respect, you should try to envisage different combinations involving urelated ideas. You should also accept external stimuli and employ the most creative and effective modes of action, in order to acquire the best possible results (prominence, lucidity of mind). Active engagement of the mind enables such stimuli to shape into views, concepts and ideas.

Seven Steps

1. To trust one's self.
2. To allow one's self the time to think.
3. To adopt a specific strategy.
4. To attempt to introduce/initiate other individuals to one's rationale and encourage them to engage in the same mode of thinking.
5. To draw a single conclusion.
6. To benefit from one's conclusion.
7. To utilise one's mode of thinking in the choice of the proper direction in life.

The most essential part is to place trust in one's own capacities. You should be able to recognise your positive attributes and achievements and be willing to defend your own beliefs.

At this point, there arises the issue of time. You should make the time to devote to certain things in life. It appears that, even though we have become quick-thinking human beings, we still lack the capacity to concentrate. Never before did individuals have so much time in their hands as today. During this century alone, people in western societies have managed to add about 25 years in their average life expectancy. In other words, we now have 50% more time to devote to the things we want to do. You should mind to render your time more productive and ascribe it with quality. Do not reach the point of having to reconsider facts over and over because of such rapid intake of information. You need time. Lack of essential time adds to individuals' mental fatigue. Psycologist Robert J. Stenberg of Yale University suggests that "the essence of intelligence would seem to be in knowing when to think and act quickly and knowing when to think and act slowly."

Moreover, goals to be achieved should be comprehensible and essentially feasible. As Descartes suggests, problems should be analysed by braking them down to their most essential elements. You should take one step at a time in order for your progress to be firm and evident. Do not take for granted anything that is not clear or tangible.

Furthermore, you should try to adjust your ideas to new information. You should not try to be perfect; instead, you should try to get better. The ultimate objective is personal improvement in a systematic, stable pace.

It is also not a good idea to attempt to find excuses for your attitude. In this way, you end up carrying them with you for life and you fail to treat other people in a simple, direct fashion. Instead, your perception is filtered by the images you have created in order to justify yourselves. Have you ever wondered if you carry such images inside you?

1.3

GET CREATIVE

Conscious thinking can be defined as the mental processes involved in determining specific goals to be achieved and strategies to be followed, as well as in devising the proper means and resources in order to acquire a desired outcome. On the other hand, unconscious mental processes relate to the state of the subconscious. Subconscious mental processes are multifold and follow a faster pace, tending to occur when they are least expected, for instance when we sleep or engage in any other relaxing activity. In moments like these, ideas strike the conscious mind in the form of enlightenment. Eventually, a process of verification is necessary to combine the conscious with the unconscious; the reality with the dream.

John Kioustelidis argues that the nature of intuition constitutes a mystery which escapes the direct attention of most of the models of memory. Intuition could be best descibed as the capacity to spontaneously devise inspirational ways of addressing situations, thereby giving solutions to problems where reasonable thinking has previously failed.

Every individual seems to possess an inner tendency towards creativity. However, if creativity lies in our nature, why are we finding it so hard to achieve? Can it be that we are insecure about ourselves or is this really a planned outcome?

In any case, we are certainly as difficult to determine and analyse and as full of vigor as every other element in the universe.

A brainstorm of spontaneous ideas

1. Take a break out of all the things you might be doing in order to devise some new ideas.
2. Focus on the matter of your concern.
3. Take a few seconds to wonder about what could be done in order to enhance or change the circumstances surrounding this subject and imagine what would happen if certain situations were different from the current state of affairs.
4. Creation. Avoid what is ordinary and try to envisage something innovative; something completely new. It is important to leave all your prejudice behind while engaging in such an attempt.
5. Think and opt for the ideas you think that might be of some worth.
6. Progress; utilise its positive and negative attributes.
7. Test your results; how is it possible to apply your ideas in an efficient way which goes beyond the ordinary?

During each of the above steps, you should mind to keep focused on your ultimate goals and try to find ways to achieve the desired outcome. It is important to think positive and not to blame yourselves in case of poor performance. It is not necessarily the case that you are unwilling to work harder to improve your capabilities. Such a negative attitude towards one's self is bound to prove the biggest impediment for future personal improvement or realisation of future plans. Hence, some of the issues to consider would be the following:

> Is it worth to engage in a certain scheme?
> How do you feel about it in the first place?
> Do you pose yourselves the right questions?
> What is your ultimate purpose?
> What is the worst thing that could happen?
> Why is this the case?
> Could you give further reasons for such circumstances?
> Have you examined creative approaches?
> What is your suggestions?
> What can you do to help futher?

One of the hardest opportunities to find is the right circumstances to try and give your best self. Therefore, you should view problems as a challenge for your capabilities and wonder whether you are likely to solve them successfully. There is no such thing in life as a period lacking concerns or difficulties. However, by adopting the proper attitude, along with positive thinking, you will be able to make a difference. After all, through the eyes of a positive individual, even strangers transform into friends. Hence, what is the worst thing that could happen?

This line of thinking is an essential part. Positive feelings boost one's energy, in contrast to negative thinking which tends to be exhausting. Excitement, happiness and effective communication with beloved people make us glow with enthusiasm. On the contrary, anger and all sorts of negative feelings exhaust us and deprive us of any positive thoughts, thereby rendering us inefficient.

It is thus advisable to give considerable attention to our dreams and objectives. On the other hand, it is preferable to release one's self from stressful situations or acquaintances.

It might be hard but it turns out to be essential for one's constitution.

Furthermore, you should try not to spoil your energy resources, by means of keeping your temper and positive attitude, rather than allowing anger to affect your frame of mind.

It is finally important to reserve an adequate amount of time for rest, in order to be able to charge your physical and emotional batteries.

> *"Intuitions result from a great deal of preparation. The moment of inspiration or illumination is when everything comes together".*
>
> Pablo Picasso

Inner self

Development of an individual's personal improvement requires such circumstances as the following:

1. Personal reaction or conscious development.
2. Why not me?   I really want to change!

3. A mentor; an individual who can advise us as to the path we should follow in life.
4. An important life experience; a life-altering event.
5. A manager.

Why is it that some people find it hard to change, unless the circumstances are suitable? Why are they finding it so hard to address things a bit different than the usual? Moreover, some people fall into the trap of identifying themselves with their problems and eventually becoming one. You should not allow past situations to hold you back. Whenever we adopt a negative attitude towards things our steps are met with resistance, which renders our course hard and painful. The solution lies, in changing one's attitude. In other words, if individuals identify themselves with negative past experiences, they allow these experiences to intervene in every aspect of their performance. It will then be hard to release themselves from the negativity involved in such a process.

In order to be able to achieve your goals, just close your eyes for a moment and think: What it is that you want to achieve? What is it that you are best capable of doing?

You can treat these questions as a self-awareness quiz, in order to get a better view of your inner world. Stop looking around you and spare a moment to just think about things you would be able to execute in the best possible way. Opt for one among them, focus on this particular one and try to analyse it. Try to figure the best way of achieving such an objective. Afterwards, think of what else you would be able to do in order to enrich it. After all, you should constantly be bearing in mind that the struggle to attain one's goals is the most tangible proof of living. Only through action are we able to hold control over our destiny and shape our future, thereby also creating a reason for living. As Henri L. Bergson suggests, you should "think like a man of action, and act like a man of thought." Do not merely wait for the right moment to act since the moment is unlikely to be perfect until your own actions render it such. Action is the breathing of one's soul. Every breath we take matters.

Key points to be taken under consideration are the following:

- Engage in activities that you feel passionate about.
- Remember that inspiration takes time.
- Conventionality rapidly comes to place and stifles innovation. Whenever you suggest an innovative idea, you should bear in mind that it is likely to be rejected by the majority of individuals.

- Engage in a lively conversation with the proper people; a conversation which is bound to include raw truths and multiple questions/views.
- Do not always seek for unanimity; unanimous decisions may not always be smart decisions.
- Determine your goals and opt for an essentially comprehensible strategy, rather than a bold one.
- Make an account of all the points that were overlooked and should have received more attention.
- Remember that there is no perfect attitude.
- Do not obstruct thought process in any possible way.
- Do not be ignorant or fail to appreciate possible risks.
- Develop your sense of humour! Greek philosopher Socrates, even when facing his trial at the age of 70 years, was still full of questions, humour and a remarkable self-awareness.
- Remember that mistakes are not to be punished but to be encouraged instead.

> *"Our doubts are traitors, and make us lose the good we oft might win by fearing to attempt".*
> William Shakespeare

Sometimes individuals ask themselves the wrong kind of questions, such as "why should this have happened to me?" Think about how much better it would be if they have wondered about their possible choices instead? Sometimes it is useful to ask one's self questions as the following:

> What are the next steps in order to prepare myself?
> How can I make something out of the currently problematic circumstances?
> What kind of opportunities may lie beneath them?
> Do other people experience the same problems?
> What do they do to solve them?

> What do successful people do when they are met
> with the same problematic circumstances?
> If there is no way to solve the problem on my own,
> where do I need to rely for help?

Remember that a problem constitutes the best occasion for your self-improvement!

The capacity to solve problems is involved in any form of human activity and is an energy demanding process. Mind not to run away from trouble, or else you will miss the chance to further develop your problem-solving strategies. You should rather attempt to address your problems directly. Treat each of them individually and examine each detail in order to figure out the proper way to solve it. Henry Ford (1863-1947) had once said that "there are no big problems; there are just a lot of little problems." In other words, a big problem is nothing but a series of smaller concerns. It is easier to examine each of the concerns separately rather that trying to address the whole problem at once. Once we get to perceive problems as opportunities for improvement, things start to change. After all, if we crave for an ocean of opportunities we must first be willing to fight with the waves.

The best thing you have to do when faced with unfortunate circumstances is to employ a healthy dose of humour. Feelings of incompetence and inability to hold control over situations constitute major sources of concern and stress. Nevertheless, a touch of humour is the first step to bring one 'back to the game'. Humour is a way to absorb life's shocks. As Francis Bacon (1561-1626) once wrote, "imagination was given to man to compensate him for what he is not; a sense of humour to console him for what he is."

1.4

PERCEPTION

"All these merely by broadening our perception . . ."

What is perception? Do we all share the same viewpoint?

Our perception of reality resembles a technique of mapping our course into life.

If we have an accurate map, we are able to know where we stand and, in case we have already decided on our course, we are able to figure out a way to reach our destination.

On the other hand, if our map is erroneous and inaccurate, we will probably end up losing our way. Although most people are well aware of such a fact, they tend to ignore it, to a more or less extent. In effect, individuals are not born with a predefined capacity to be able to identify their life-course, but rather figure their way into life in the long run. This is a highly demanding process and some people are unwilling to make such an effort. Therefore, their maps are often small and draft and their worldview tends to be restricted and misleading. Our perception of reality indeed resembles a map; different maps give rise to different worldviews, different attitudes and different approaches.

Perception is shaped out of information emanating from human senses. Although all of the senses are capable of equally contributing to the construction of individuals' perception, merely one of them is often enough to generate the same effect.

The only means to achieve a competitive advantage is through acquisition of brand new knowledge or a different viewpoint which will give rise to insightful ideas. Individuals who adopt a different viewpoint, proceed to innovative creation, and share their knowledge are worthy of lot more than any asset.

Individuals' worldview is defined by their own constitution and personality. We all have different talents and capabilities, as well as our own personal limits. This is how things go. You should be able to identify your own strengths and weaknesses. In this way, you will be able to enhance your performance by empowering your strengths and treating your weaknesses appropriately. Among the factors to influence one's perception is attitude, various interests, past experiences and finally life prospects and expectations.

When attached to past experiences, individuals often rely on previous achievements over and over again, counting on the experience they assume to have acquired out of them. Nevertheless, a different approach is often required to attain one's objectives and this is where experience impedes further progress. In this respect, it would be prudent to change one's way of thinking. Times change and they should give rise to generations with different ideas and viewpoints. Have you ever considered that your own viewpoint might not be appropriate for your times? No change—might that be internal or external—can be sustained, unless it is followed by a deeper revaluation of one's way of thinking. It is thus advisable to consciously try and keep yourselves in good shape. It is important to get as much sleep as you need and avoid negative or straining circumstances.

Likewise, you also need to attend to your spirit. Keep your mind on alert, think positive and attempt to figure plausible solutions to your problems, in order to shape the best possible circumstances for your everyday life. Love yourselves and have faith in your capabilities. Keep cultivating the abilities which will give prominence to your talents. If you keep performing your duties in the best possible way, change is likely to visit you soon.

Four steps to acquire the driving force for change

Conscience operates on four levels in order to allow individuals to distinguish between appropriate and inappropriate circumstances.

First comes the emotional factor which is followed by a sense of fatigue, particularly when it fails to provide satisfaction in everyday life professional or personal affairs.

What follows is introspection which allows individuals to determine the factor causing inconvenience. It is the second step to one's attempt to change in order to attain a desired outcome.

Moreover, it is important to thoroughly examine one's self in order to discover the parameters which offer the most satisfaction and thirst for life.

It is also crucial to have faith and trust one's self. Remember that inspiration requires time; hence, it is not advisable to rush into things. Allow your thought and time become one.

If you are still hesitant, remember that when a groundbreaking idea comes into question, most of the people reject it. Therefore, you should rely upon your own uniqueness.

Thought process

Thought process evolves around eight frames of positive thinking aiming at progress and development. It is only after distinguishing between these different levels that we are able to further improve them.

The first frame of thought regards our desires and the extent to which we wish for change and improvement. It is probably the most essential among the different levels/steps of any thought process. Additionally, this frame also includes the extent to which we are aware of the things we aspire to change or enhance. In any case, alertness serves as one's own radar.

Individuals should always seek for new paths in life; they should observe, compare and contrast and then revaluate their current views. Nothing is to be taken for granted; we should constantly seek to weave new circumstances.

We are living in times ever-changing; in times of intense rhythms where everything moves in exceedingly high speed. We have been forced to think fast and act even faster, often overlooking most of the abovementioned principles.

What for?

Negative frames of thought process

One's habits often constitute a point of criticism and allow for further enhancement. Some of them are even revised and changed at some point, such as the ones which consume a lot of valuable time to be devoted to more creative or productive activities. It should be mentioned that recreational activities are not included in this very last category.

It is only natural that individuals consider other people's view regarding their own attitude and mode of living. This is a point which requires change, or at least some extent of control. Cowardice has no place in this process. How often do you lie in bed regretting about things you never did or opportunities you missed? Life is too short and you have got to live it! You need to have faith in yourselves and trust your own judgment. Courage and self-confidence are only essential in order to achieve change in your way of living, your attitude and the way other people behave to you. Lack of self-confidence is an issue to be addressed efficiently.

Moreover, it is important to be active, in terms of both lifestyle and mental functions. Lack of mental activity is equal to reluctance of abandoning the past. On the contrary, rapid thinking and alertness are signs of eagerness to move to the future. Therefore, these are attributes to be cultivated and enhanced.

1.5

PERSONAL BENCHMARKING

Benchmark is another word for a point of reference. In terms of marketing, benchmarking is associated with certain steps and directions which are followed—or should be followed—by a company in order to achieve enhanced performance in a number of areas, including improvement of the conditions of marketing channels, or even sales; in other words, strategies which are bound to render the company a point of reference in its domain of activity.

Would you ever shoot at someone without having attempted to aim accurately in the first place? If you really wanted to hit them then the answer is probably no. Likewise, the routine of living in contemporary societies encourage individuals to only proceed to actions that please them, rather than what is best for them. This kind of attitude comes with a price we they eventually have to pay.

Choosing thoughtless action over conscientious behaviour can only lead to dreams being forever lost and may go as far as to cause some sort of emotional disorder.

Constant creation must be and end in its own right, along with the discovery of a new path to improvement.

What follows is a definition of benchmarking and its different stages, in order to introduce us more effectively to the concept of observing only what is best and trying to achieve enhanced performance.

BENCHMARKING

Benchmarking is the process of comparing the products, services, targets and operations of a firm to primary rival firms in its industry, or to firms which claim the throne of king in their domain of activity. On an individual basis, benchmarking is the constant, systematic process of comparing one's self to other people who have been acknowledged as experts in a given field. What we all should do is attempt to identify the strengths of such individuals, as well as the nature of their superiority. Developing one's observation skills is probably the most valuable asset out of the process of benchmarking.

Benchmarking as a circular process of improvement

If you attempt to render the above-mentioned definition more personal or anthropocentric, you will come to the conclusion that you should focus on what other people do best and try to imitate their actions. Nevertheless, who is to determine that other individuals do the right thing? Who is to guarantee that by observing their actions you will be able to overcome them in excellence and be the first in your domain?

According to the concept of benchmarking, individuals enhance their performance by comparing themselves to certain standards. On the other hand, such an attitude might not be suitable and effective when it comes to multidimensional situations. A successful attempt is often not enough to guarantee future success under different circumstances. Hence, following the strategies of benchmarking is not enough to render us superior; in this way we are just limited to following other people's line of action.

The Samurai in pre-industrial Japan were distinguished for creating their own laws and principles, among other reasons. Even today, Japanese people have embraced and adjusted such values to their contemporary way of living, namely the *daimyo*. The samurai never followed other people's steps. They made their own way to creation until they reached the point of perfection; that is, *dadotsu*, as they named it. It is the ultimate purpose to be attained through constant effort to refine themselves and reach perfection.

Likewise, classic philosophers attended to human beings as creatures with the capacity to develop and fully realise themselves for the ultimate purpose of reaching perfection.

For some people, inner development leads to harmony, in the sense of inward tranquillity, an ending to one's journey, balance, serenity, or peace. This is what they visualise and such is their life purpose. Sometimes it might be a fairly good strategy to look around you, think for a moment and try to figure out what you most expect out of life, releasing yourselves from thoughts of competition and the feeling of hastiness.

In order to be able to lead yourselves first and then other individuals as well, you need to be familiar with the cycle of your personal change. In other words, it is necessary to analyse your own thoughts, both of emotional and of psychological nature, and have the courage and modesty required to discuss your ideas with friends, colleagues and other people who hold you in high esteem, in order to eventually be able to study their reactions. Naturally, such a process requires that you are surrounded by individuals who have some extent of moral standards, in order to be able to judge properly. You should attempt to establish a culture where freedom of speech encourages the expression of disagreement or difference. By means of studying your own ideas, you will eventually be able to look further than your own perception. Moreover, you will be able to recognise given circumstances and create something new, or enhance yourselves and your current thoughts.

A real leader must be a researcher at the same time. Effectiveness at this point calls for the attitude and the practices of an open-minded individual with the will to experiment.

Look around you; observe, study given circumstances and reconsider your attitude.

Changing one's attitude

People change attitude when:

- They recognise their weaknesses.
- They aspire to improve themselves.
- The circumstances are suitable.
- They receive help from others.
= They are given the opportunity to adopt new modes of attitude.

You should not pay attention to other people's mistakes; you should rather focus on what you can do which might be of help to other people, irrespective of whether they are willing to help you in return. The moment you decide to give someone a second chance is the moment when a leader is born. Remember that it is better to think of leadership as attitude, rather than a certain role you are required to fulfil.

The trap

Why should I bother changing my ways if they have led me to success in the past?

In a world of constant variation, idleness is not an option. Individuals often need to change the way they operate according to given circumstances, since past conditions are not to be taken for granted. Life would be much too convenient if we could get things done employing the same old strategies no matter the circumstances.

Attitude

What drives people towards change?

1. It might be the case of too much strain . . .
They have overanalysed the same situations for too long that they eventually decide they can take no more. They have bet so many times on the same horse that they finally decide to give up.

2. Among the driving forces for change is this mild form of despair which takes the form of tediousness; dullness; boredom. This is often the case with individuals who keep waiting for more convenient circumstances, asking themselves 'now what'? When this question becomes overwhelming, they know it is the right time for change.

3. Individuals might also want to change just because they suddenly came to realise such a possibility.

4. Finally, unfortunate situations often make people adopt a whole new different perspective in life. In times like these it is not necessary to seek for change, since change has already occurred in the form of surrounding circumstances.

Jaspers argues that we are gradually moved to change from a state of everyday routine; in other words, a situation where individuals are motivated to change their way of living after an overwhelming, irreversible experience which leads them to a more genuine state of existence.

"Somebody should tell us, right at the start of our lives that we are dying. Then we might live life to the limit, every minute of every day. Do it I say! Whatever you want to do, do it now! There are only so few tomorrows!" When Michael Landon said these words, he knew he would probably die young. And so it happened. Still, he had the chance to become a director, an actor, a writer and a producer. Individuals who opt for action, opt for life itself; a life fully realised through an active lifestyle. It is always possible to choose between action and idleness, in the same way as we choose between doing the right or wrong thing. We can always do the proper actions and make ourselves feel well.

Experience is there to teach us the limits of our current actions, as well as the extent to which they can stretch. The more we remain idle the more we sink in the quicksand of idleness. On the other hand, inappropriate actions can hold us back in the same way proper actions can lift us high. In other words, idleness gradually leads to paralysis whereas action leads to progress. As Robert Schuller puts it, "winning starts with beginning."

Creativity lies in the very nature of human beings. On the other hand, we can cultivate our creativity by shaping our own selves and performing deeds of courage. On that account, individual performance depends on the following parameters:

1. Your own self and personality.

    You should exploit every opportunity to cultivate your personality by means of reading, acquiring information and improving your relationships with other people. Emotions such as insecurity, selfishness, ambition, greed and luck of trust play an important role in personal improvement.
2. Mode of operation when working with other individuals.

You should aim at improving your knowledge, attitude and relationship with other people.
3. Overall mode of operation.
Your mode of operation requires constant revaluation and improvement. By attending to the abovementioned parameters, you are also expected to improve:
4. Your work.

Keep in mind that the person you currently are is determined and controlled by your good and bad habits. As Aristotle mentions, "We are what we repeatedly do. Excellence, then, is not an act, but a habit." This means, then, that our habits shape our nature. Repeated patterns of action come to be consolidated as habits, which form our character and implicitly define our future. Hence, what is required to change is not power of will but a thorough comprehension of our habits.

Time for change and decision making

It is now the right time to change your attitude, as well as reconsider certain features of your behaviour.

In which way?

You first need to be able to identify them. You should observe your response to various stimuli, along with your reactions to certain people. Release yourselves from prejudice and seek to comprehend real communication messages.

Time for training

You should take advantage of every occasion to train yourselves appropriately. Training may come from one's experience, workplace or various readings. Seek to read as much as you can and acquire useful information.

Nietzsche's aphorism that what matters is not individuals' courage to stay true to their beliefs but rather the strength to change these beliefs, sounds really interesting in that concept. After all, this is what life is all about; change. Variation ascribes life with meaning and contributes to its natural flow.

Entropy, on the other hand, is a force which opposes to individuals' capacity to change. The more the extent of entropy, the less the probability of achieving considerable variation.

Basic principle of dialectics:

Thesis + Antithesis = Synthesis
Thesis − Antithesis = Decomposition

In the above equation, thesis corresponds to your own attitude/view and antithesis to the respective attitude/view of your interlocutor. As two distinct individuals, you are expected to equally contribute in order to bridge your differences and come up with a new relationship which will lead to synthesis. The opposite is the case of conflict, which is far from being creative. Instead, it is a form of decomposition and a rather unfortunate attempt to construct a different opinion or relationship.

1.6

IMPROVING ONE'S ATTITUDE

How is it possible to change and improve one's attitude? To what extent do you exhibit an 'elasticity of behaviour'?

Elasticity of behaviour

Elasticity of behaviour regards the nature of individuals' respond to different people and circumstances. It may sound simple, but think of how many of us exhibit recurrent patterns of behaviour when it comes to particular people and situations.

How easy would it be to change one's established behaviour towards other people, for instance colleagues? It is certainly not as easy as it sounds. Think of how many things go through your mind on an ordinary day and your respective reactions to everyday life occurrences.

Some people have learned to exhibit a sort of 'automatic response' and have become effective when it comes to situations like driving or other everyday operations. Nevertheless, mind that life consists of a series of unique moments which determine our existence through time. Have you ever wondered with what criteria you would like to determine the crucial moments in your everyday life? How is it possible to control your reaction to situations in order to make the decisions you really mean to? Answers to these questions may once again appear simple but are the ones to define our future over and over again. It is through such choices that we are able to come closer to our energy potential and thereby change and become more creative.

Moreover, each action is followed by a series of consequences, may these be positive or negative. Therefore, you should consider what you can possibly obtain out of your every move. Afterwards, you may compare the positive and negative attributes, in order to be able to distinguish which of your objectives worth the most.

In any case, you should decide on what is important for you and seek to prioritise. Make sure that your work does not contradict your values. Remember that the energy you invest in a given activity emanates from your own energy potential.

Ask yourselves first

Do you think you are ready to handle particular situations in particular ways? Do you unconsciously exhibit the same behaviour whenever someone comes to you with a particular problem? It appears that, when acting against their own will, individuals tend to unconsciously adopt recurring patterns of attitude.

In such cases, it might be useful to consider if you carry experiences which are likely to justify your (recurrent) reactions to certain events. As we are gradually getting exposed, we tend to adopt certain excuses for our attitude. Hence, such attitudes gradually turn to consolidated patterns of behaviour and often affect our perception regarding other people, since the last one is filtered by distorted images we constructed ourselves in order to justify our actions. We tend to expose ourselves whenever our thoughts and feelings comply with the excuses we find for our attitude. In this way we also tend to exaggerate when it comes to other people's defects and put the blame on them for any fault that we do, at the same time highlighting our own positive attributes. Stressing other people's weaknesses merely to make ourselves feel better is improper. It is worth mentioning that it is such 'established' modes of conduct which eventually come to label our actions and affect our reputation, since individuals are determined by their own attitude and deeds.

Therefore, you should try to eliminate any signs of respective behaviour in your everyday operations. You should rather treat other people as individuals with whom you share the same essential needs, hopes and concerns.

Habits—established patterns of behaviour

You might have caught yourselves thinking, at times, that you could have adopted a more suitable approach to a given situation. If only you had attended to things from a positive viewpoint, rather than being ill-disposed to other individuals, you might have adopted a different treatment. It is thus worth trying new attitudes and conducts in order to figure out which of them are the most effective and which can only prove unfruitful.

Several issues should be considered at this point. The first problem is that much of our reactions occur in an 'autopilot mode'; that is, we tend to unconsciously react to certain stimuli before having the chance to mentally negotiate our attitude in the first place, much like our body's striking response when it comes to external threats. Under the circumstances, we end up making mistakes, since we were not ready to act accordingly in the first place. Nevertheless, you should not be discouraged. A life without mistakes resembles a lecture theatre with no lectures. Remember these words: "Life is hard . . . thank you God!"

Try and adopt a more genuine attitude towards other people, may these be familiar to you or total strangers. If you embrace them all, it is only to be expected that your attitude will be positive and unpretentious. It will also come natural; with a smile.

On the other hand, you should be prepared for the sort of attitude you are likely to receive on the part of other individuals, since you might need to adopt a slightly more moderate behaviour. Hasty reactions often fail to meet a positive outcome. Instead, you should consider taking some time to think over your reactions and act on the basis of more calculated moves than the ones you would have probably thought in the first place. The same applies to various problems or unfortunate circumstances which often put our endurance into test.

Mind that, when you come to familiarise with your actual feelings, you need to be careful as to your respective reactions. Your actions must be dictated by reason, rather than by your unreasonable impulses. At first, this is a rather challenging scheme, resembling the attempt to get used to breathing through your diaphragm rather than your nose. Moreover, it constitutes a twofold choice; you either choose your own destination or settle with being a mere passenger with no idea of how far the journey goes and when it is going to end. Indeed, in no case does this mean that feelings and emotions are necessarily an enemy. They might as well prove to be a negative influence but they can also be of help according to given circumstances.

It follows that only when individuals are really conscious about their actions they are ready to move towards change. It is all up to you. Make your dreams and ideas reality. Set targets and ascribe your life with a sense of meaning and purpose. Enrich your experiences and take pleasure out of every moment. At the same time, you should mind what is important in your life. This might include making a difference in the lives of other people by being a good friend and a source of inspiration. After all, acknowledgement, understanding and acceptance are what most individuals look for in life. You can prove other people how important they are to you by giving them what they want most. You can be certain that your positive energy and encouraging words will have a striking effect upon them.

Furthermore, you should take advantage of every opportunity and lay the foundation for realising your dreams and goals in life. It is important to defend your beliefs and rights, as well as those of other individuals. Do not hesitate to express your enthusiasm on the grounds of criticism. Instead, you can pave the way for other people as well.

Organisational development consultant Jill Janov confirms that it is better to think of leadership as an attitude, rather than a role. The more attentive you are as to your actions the more you are going to be rewarded. You should also bear in mind that, in trying to improve your capacities, you are bound to meet obstacles in the form of resistance to the undermining of your current identity. It is thus useful to treat the situation by reminding yourselves that the new 'you' might destroy your current self, but will resemble more the person you want to become/your true self; therefore, you will not give up trying. Refuse to settle with the same old situations which might eventually render you incapable of achieving essential change.

If you are still unhappy with the attained outcome, try to increase your self-control. Ask yourselves if there is anything you could do differently in order to come up with better results. Potential failure is not something to be dreaded. You might as well gain a useful experience out of it, since it gives you the opportunity to further develop your courage. Citing Confucius' words, "the greatest glory in living lies not in never falling, but in rising every time we fall." After all, only the ones who never try are the ones who never fail. In effect, success is about never giving up. It is, thus, better to make an effort to do something and fail rather than not try at all in the first place. Bear in mind that there are three kinds of people: the ones who try to make something happen, the ones who sit back and watch and those who keep wondering what everything is all about. If only you aspire to fall into the first category, you are expected to take risks and make a meaningful effort. Remember: When you are not happy with the attained outcome, try to increase your self-control and go for it again.

PART II

2.1

MANAGEMENT IN TIMES OF CRISIS

Introduction

There is a plethora of theoretical books out there addressing management of human resources and responsibilities, in order to help organisations perform in the best possible way. Be that as it may, only a few of them suggest actual ways of applying what is written to everyday situations. This particular book constitutes a valuable tool in managers' attempt to put the basic principles of management into action in the workplace.

In this work, several methods are examined and theories are applied into practical contexts. Throughout its pages, a different style of management is easily discernible; one which is explicit and effective, associating different theories with employees who have worked hard to maintain the high standards of a company.

In order to apply the content of the book into real-life situations, you need to be focused to the objectives you have specified, thereby also implicitly realising your vision. Such a scheme requires accurate planning of one's time and available resources, as well as determination to acquire the desired objective. Determination does not necessarily imply a change in one's planning, except for situations which call for such modifications. Otherwise, leaders might overlook underlying antagonists or other factors causing delays in the whole scheme. Still, despite the parameters specified above, leaders'/managers' devotion to their objectives, as well as final success cannot be guaranteed. Nevertheless, they are most likely to be attained, to a certain extent.

A combination of such principles with the proper values transforms leaders' goal to a vision for their people. In harsh times and conditions, management should at least be effective. It might be true that theories regarding human resources apply before and after a period of crisis, but rarely is this the case during the actual crisis. At this point, human resources and HR policies, as well as training programmes are of a rather secondary importance. The primary concern lies in the survival of the company and the strategies to avoid the impact of the crisis.

Recruitment

Apart from a daily routine, the process of seeking for the appropriate candidate constitutes an essential process, from structuring the proper vacancy announcement to the final interview. This process alone is enough to judge the efficiency of a team and, by extension, that of the overall organisation.

A vacancy announcement must be cohesive in its structure and accurate as to the description of the candidate wanted. Ideally, it should attract the attention of the suitable candidates only, rather than leading in a pile of irrelevant and tiresome CVs which require an equally tedious processing. Therefore, as soon as you gather the CVs for a particular vacancy announcement, you might find useful to divide them into three categories:

- The positive. These are the ones which gather positive attributes, such as related studies, seminars, foreign languages, previous experience and any other requirement an employee is expected to meet in order to be suitable for the job.
- The moderate. This is the right place to put the CVs of candidates, for which you have not yet formed a definite impression. There might be features which sound appealing and others which are not as encouraging as to convince you to call them for an interview. Therefore, you probably need time to make the right decision. In effect, such a category is also necessary in case you do not gather enough positive CVs and need to resolve to the less appealing options.
- The negative. These are CVs that leave a lot to be desired. Such candidates might lack the necessary qualification or have skills which are irrelevant to the specific job position. It follows that these kinds of CVs are also the ones not expected to appear in your lists.

After the vacancy announcement has been structured, the next step is preparation for the stage 2; interviews. When you have finally decided on the appropriate candidates, you should be properly prepared to test their abilities in the most effective fashion, preferably by means of behavioural interviews and psychometric tests. As regards the last ones, there are plenty of questions on the internet which can help you prepare your interview. Otherwise, you could consult a specialised company, in order to prepare more effectively. These kinds of tests constitute a powerful tool in shaping the desired team or company and examine knowledge of emotional intelligence, body language and any principle essential to the particular job. It might also be useful to construct a set of sub questions to supplement the principle ones. In any case, you should be attentive to any of the candidates' reactions and keep notes throughout the process, provided that you have asked for their permission at the beginning of the interview.

During an interview, what is of primary interest to you is associated to the candidates themselves, rather than the rest of the group they might have worked with in the past. Therefore, you should be looking for personal assertions, rather than descriptions of collective achievements. Moreover, if you expect your employees to hold values as individuals, you must be interested in specific tactics that led them to their various achievements. You might want to examine whether they have attained their goals by legitimate means—also proving that they are more skilled—or in cooperation with other people, possible also utilising illegitimate means.

Furthermore, along with the CVs, it is advisable to keep appropriate notes concerning your candidates, as this is likely to help you decide whether it is worth meeting them more than once. During these meetings, you need to make the right questions and compare and contrast their answers. In effect, you should mind to schedule the interviews with a distance of at least ten days in between. This is a useful tactics, since most candidates start feeling more relaxed as soon as they are familiar to their surrounding environment. Therefore, they might provide you with information which they had failed to mention the previous times.

Ideally, the above-mentioned strategies will help you employ the candidate who best suits your criteria. A final piece of advice at this point: opt for individuals with a high degree of emotional intelligence and passion. The first element is essential in order to shape a team of members who will perform together in harmony and the second is likely to lead in greater effort and higher performances on their part.

2.2

TRAINING

What follows the recruitment of appropriate candidates is their orientation to the company/organisation in question. By the time candidates are introduced in the workplace, they must be trained to conform to essential principles within the organisation, in order to be able to perform in the proper way. A key element of success at this stage is the manager/supervisor, who is also expected to serve as a consultant to the new employees.

The second stage in the process is called product training and concerns the specific duties the candidate is expected to execute. The more accurate the training, the more productive the candidate is likely to be, thereby also avoiding making lots of mistakes.

Furthermore, the candidate needs to receive adequate training in order to learn to conform to the values of the organisation. Such values, along with the overall culture of the organisation, are inviolable laws for the workforce. New candidates may be used to different attitudes, work pace or performance requirements. Moreover, they might not be familiar with teamwork, or exhibit several other attitudes which do not comply with the policy of their new workplace. Therefore, proper training and instruction as to the rules of the particular organisation help to avoid improper conducts which may lead in conflict among the employees. In other words, the candidate is expected to leave the past behind and adjust to the reality of the new workplace.

Culture

In one of my previous works, *Leadership Today*, there is a chapter devoted to the definition and the crucial importance of culture in terms of an organisation or a single team. Culture is what characterises different organisations and provides the motivation for better performance among the employees. It is also closely associated with the level of education, either on an individual or on an overall basis. It consists in the overall values, beliefs and attitudes of an individual or a group of individuals. Organisational culture consists in the attitudes of the employees regarding issues that affect the company or them individually, which are mainly dictated by the level of their education.

It follows that culture is something which cannot be perceived with a naked eye. According to Edgar Schein[1] of MIT, culture is a model of basic principles which aims at helping individuals to resolve issues of external adjustment and internal integration, or unity. It has been so well constructed and applied that it is considered valid. Therefore, new members of an organisation embrace a given culture model and uti-

---

[1] Organizational Culture and Leadership, Edgar Schein, John Wiley & Sons, Inc. 2004

lise it as a basis for thought and perception of various issues within the workplace. Such issues include the way in which employees may handle a decline in profit, their different concerns within the workplace, lack of information on the part of the administration, or the psychoemotional impact that certain external or internal changes of setting and conducts within the organisation have upon the workforce. Moreover, it may also be the case of the way in which higher executives or departments react to the innovative or different ideas of subordinate employees, according to the position of the last ones in the organisation. Employees in organisations which operate on the basis of a strong culture instinctively prioritise according to the importance of issues to be resolved and adopt the same viewpoint over market operations and treatment of various situations.

Culture is essential to management operations and shaping a proper culture is of core importance to an organisation. Culture functions as a sort of saving grace during harsh market conditions, resolving unfortunate circumstances and eventually releasing the organisation from the burden. In other words it is the basis for a positive treatment and appropriate response, according to the gravity of a matter. Hence, in an organisation, whose culture is in harmony with the intended outcome, employees assume prompt reaction to given circumstances. In the opposite case, the organisation ends up passively adopting any change that might be necessary.

As regards leaders of organisations, not only do they have to inspire the workforce due to their knowledge and actions, but they also need to be severe and show zero tolerance to attitudes contrasting the culture within the organisation. Justice must appear to be objective and impartial; anything pointing to the opposite direction must be eliminated. It lies in the responsibility of leaders and their managers to support and safeguard such rightfulness within the organisation.

Individuals who have successfully undergone the interview part and are finally called to work for an organisation are expected to respect the values and attitudes dictated by given leaders, in order to attain the best possible outcome in the near future. This is much like a professional soccer player competing in a different field than the one he was used to; at some point he will probably need to change his tactics.

In order for the culture of an organisation to be shaped, the leader has to decide upon what will be expected from the workforce. If what is primarily required is knowledge, he or she should opt for candidates with a variety of qualifications in their CVs, along with a high level of ambition. If, nevertheless, the weight should be laid upon determination, the appropriate candidates are individuals, whose values will give rise to respective attitudes in the workplace. Skills, such as speed, if manipulated properly on the part of the leader, may lead in a high competitive advantage. At the same time, each value has to be examined under a specific framework, may that be time or anything else. In this respect, speed constitutes the relatively rapid pace at which various information pass through one department to another. Without a specific framework, only a few of the employees are likely to transform such values into established attitudes. Hence, each of them is bound to work at their own individual pace, a factor of much inconvenience to heads of departments, particularly within exceedingly competitive markets.

No value is capable of leading an organisation to success in its own right. It takes more to realise such a scheme, such as cooperation and honesty. Lack of cooperation between different departments or teams often leads to significant delay and thereby also to loss of valuable opportunities. Likewise, lack of honesty impedes recovery from mistaken moves of the past and increases the possibility of repetition in the future. Therefore, it is only reasonable that managers and leaders must be rigid as to compliance with the values of the organisation. Unless values transform into established patterns of attitude, no means is available for shaping a respective culture. If such values are shaped into proper modes of conduct, it will be easy to attain a highly competitive organisation with a consistent policy embraced by the whole of the workforce.

A final point of concern for a manager/leader, regarding the issue of culture, is the sense of community they are expected to promote within the workplace.

2.3

HEROES; THE LEADERS OF TOMORROW

According to bibliographic literature, a hero is a strong and courageous individual; one who is distinguished for noble deeds and a bravery that stretches to the limits of self-sacrifice. Moreover, it is usually taken for granted that a hero's constitution is permeated by a law of honour and moral principles. Therefore, they are held as model figures for the rest of the society. Heroes 'play with their cards open' and rarely give rise to criticism concerning their tactics. They feel different than the rest of the people, not in an arrogant fashion but rather in a sense of daring to argue with anyone and distinguish themselves from the crowd in a straightforward manner, yet without assuming a provocative attitude. Furthermore, they usually do not resolve in forming factions within the workplace or employing any other underhand means, but rather attempt to bring change with their own attitude.

The promotion of such individuals, in or out of the framework of an organisation, lies in the duties of given leaders, who are responsible for shaping such characters and providing them with opportunities to unfold their talents, in order to eventually rise into model figures within the microcosm of the organisation. This is not the only case where leaders are required to undertake certain responsibilities on their own. They usually find themselves assuming twofold duties; that of both a manager and a leader, at the same time inspiring their people.

Today's leaders are expected to make their way 'through the fire and flames'. Current crisis causes considerable variations in and out of the framework of organisations. Skills to be developed for immediate use would be best described as survival mechanisms, particularly in cases where leaders had acquired such capabilities in the past and are now called to put them in practice, in order to be distinguished in their field of activity.

On the other hand, tomorrow's leaders will need to demonstrate that they have struggled all the way to their position. Current circumstances are tougher and more complex than past conditions, primarily due to the financial crisis that has permeated the market and households. Hence, the one who struggles in such a chaotic reality might as well be considered a hero. Likewise, the one who has been shaken without falling down is a hero. The word 'hero' may sound weird at this context, but one should consider that, from a state of past abundance, significant parts of the population—employees, families, citizens—have now been reduced to deprivation. The rate of unemployment keeps rising on a daily basis, rendering the situation even more unfortunate. Therefore, such circumstances suffice to justify an increasingly aggressive and demanding environment.

What would be the answer to the crisis then?

A possible solution would be a higher supply of services, along with intense effort, speed and cooperation among the different departments. In any case, information in such cases is of core importance. It follows that, if information holders/providers were 'ahead of the game' before, in times of crisis they seem to be invincible. This is yet another element constructing the personality of a leader; holding the proper information in order to proceed to striking action when socio-economic circumstances allow so.

Indeed, all the above presuppose that a working team will develop the proper reflexes in order to be able to follow the leader. An analogy could be drawn between the work team and a well-trained army force, strategically aligned in order to survive the fight unharmed. People today are forced to go through a fight; a sort of often unfair and immoral struggle which exceeds personal limits yet requires individuals to come out of the battle as winners.

What current organisations lack is leaders who struggle their way into success and need to keep doing so, whether they are active in politics or in a big organisation for the common good. Individuals who take chances in the middle of today's crisis undergo a 'Herculean task'. Hence, a new model of leader is developed out of current circumstances.

One could argue that the basic prerequisite underlying the existence of a hero is actual war or crisis conditions. The current crisis, which employees undergo, is a different type of war. People who have been made redundant and struggle with financial difficulties end up losing their ability to socialise and are forced to reconsider their needs and dreams in life. Some people's plans for marriage and kids are indefinitely postponed. As with any other form of crisis, the financial instability gives rise to various fears and insecurities. The sense of security is one of the vital factors affecting individuals' emotional state. In times of crisis, such a feeling is lost and replaced by the impression of constant change and variation. People find it hard to resolve such issues and feel like they are losing control. Principal feelings involved are stress, fear, insecurity, anxiety, nervousness, anger and a sense of general disorder. Chronic stress is a condition which affects individuals' immune system, rendering them more vulnerable to physical or emotional illnesses, at the same time causing their gradual surrender ("I am incapable of reacting"). The consequences of such a condition vary. They can go from questioning one's efficiency, isolation, and as far as causing disorder to social and familial relationships.

In the past, heroes were distinguished for their strength, courage and bravery which could stretch to self-sacrifice, if necessary. Nowadays, the principles that form a heroic personality lie in the ability to struggle in the midst of a chaotic environment, at the same time caring about one's people and country. Heroes are also expected to be intelligent and effectively overcome any struggle. Today's hero resembles David, rather than Goliath.

Today's heroes are the ones who have suffered misfortunes without giving up and have finally managed to overcome them. Such could be employees who managed to combat redundancy or businesspeople who managed not to proceed in dismissals of workforce. Furthermore, they are the ones who struggle employing legitimate means and finally manage to survive. They are capable of acquiring the best possible results due to their sharpness, creativity and innovation.

In the setting of business, heroes have faith in the organisation and the leadership. They go the extra mile for the benefit of the organisation and remain faithful to leaders, minding to provide them with a detailed account of the current circumstances. Moreover, their actions are characterised by high ethics and integrity all the way. They manage to live through everyday events, attaining desired change and avoiding being manipulated. Further qualities of their personality are psychological strength, self-control, diligence, patriotism and adequate knowledge. These attributes help them to become the leaders of tomorrow.

Today's leaders promote the image of heroes as model figures to be followed. They support them and train them. They mentor them, care to introduce them to positive and hopeful circumstances and try to create the atmosphere of a community. In other words, the leaders aim at communicating the idea of putting duty and the best interest of the organisation over individual pursuits.

The above-mentioned principles contribute to the rising of a new leadership style within a business setting. The leaders of tomorrow must be the heroes of current times. Leaders currently struggle employing legitimate means, try to cut down on the expenses instead of the workforce, enhance their skills out of whatever chaotic situation they go through, develop a sense of insight for future circumstances and end up being embraced by the whole of the workforce in the organisation.

In terms of politics, future leaders must also be heroes of current times. They should be well informed as to issues of globalisation and hold a high level of overall education. They should also preferably be around the age of 40 to 45 and be already successful in their current profession. Furthermore, political leaders should be heroic enough to be able to judge and negotiate over important matters and struggle for the interest of their country. They should hold high morals and be highly concerned about the notions of democracy and solidarity.

New heroes rising out of today's crisis are meant to constitute the leaders of tomorrow.

2.4

MANAGEMENT

Management is concerned with human resources and the constitution of the workforce, at the same time involving issues of proper function of the organisation. Managers are responsible for recruiting and training the appropriate people in such a way as to be able to achieve the intended goals of the team or the organisation (both quantitative and qualitative).

Generally, the success of a manager/leader lies in one, sole choice: whether they really want to succeed or not. If they aspire to be efficient, they are expected to overcome their fears and prove that they are the ones who construct the rules in the first place.

In this book, no distinction is made between leaders and managers (as in similar books one might have read) since heads of departments and directors are expected to either lead or manage their subordinate employees according to given circumstances. It is the circumstances alone that often define the position of leaders and managers. In an interview for the New York Times, president and chief executive officer of Symantec Enrique Salem mentioned that "[m]anaging means sometimes you've got to deliver a tough message. But you've got to give the feedback in a way that has a constructive tone." It follows that, if only do managers aspire to save the organisation from crisis, they need to be realistic and avoid sentimentalism.

2.5

THE LEADER; YOU

At this point, you might want to decide on your intended external image, in order to form your attitude according to such aspirations. You may first want to figure a way of achieving this goal, as well as the suitable means. Your next step must be to pay attention to people you communicate with and observe their reactions. If their response is not the one you would expect, you should change your attitude and try again.

Communication is a vital point of friction with other people; therefore, we should be constantly trying to enhance it until we reach the point of perfection. Such implies various changes and a lot of consideration of the suitable channels for communication, in case it comes out to be ineffective. Mind not to encourage attitudes on the part of other individuals, for which you may have been criticising them in the first place.

In order to acquire better responses from yourselves or other people, you should be more attentive to their reactions, sensitive to their emotions and at the same time also cautious as to your own self-awareness. You should be concerned about offering help to others, rather than receiving their own support. Quite a few individuals do not care to help their colleagues, even though they actually know that this is probably what they should be doing. The Golden Rule requires us to get into other people's position and try to imagine how they feel.

The above concepts are not abstract. They can be promoted and cultivated within a healthy environment, as well as vanish during times of fear and insecurity.

Furthermore, quite a few people are poor listeners and there are even more poor observers. They get confused and lose their temper when other individuals do not understand them or do not react in the expected manner. It follows that the ability to observe other individuals' reactions and listen to their words is essential. You need to pay attention to detail; every single utterance and the way it is phrased. Body language, pitch and facial expressions of the interlocutor are crucial in determining whether you have adopted the proper attitude and whether you have attained the desired outcome. In final analysis, a leader must be embraced by other people in the team or organisation.

Leadership is divided in two parts: official and unofficial. Official leadership is determined and appointed by given boards of directors—in the case of companies/organisations—or by the body of citizens—in the case of elections. In other words, official leadership is the officially appointed leadership. On the other hand, unofficial leadership may not be officially appointed but is commonly acceptable by the majority of individuals. Unofficial leadership policies are constructed out of certain attitudes which aim at helping other people/colleagues, without expecting anything in return. They are also determined by expertise in a professional field.

A general advice would be to be willing to give to other people and not to keep everything to yourselves. Do not hesitate to share knowledge and positive attitudes, or give others more that they would expect. Such an attitude is likely to render you respectful and add up to your status. Your lifestyle should resemble a flame which is gradually nourished by proper attitudes and knowledge in such a way as to improve your external image.

Unfortunately, today's leaders do not provide individuals with a distinct sense of values or clear directions, in a way to make them feel part of a community with a broader sense of purpose; one that inspires them and brings them close to millions of other people, in order to unite in a common effort. It turns out that individuals are treated as mere means, rather than the core point of concern for their leaders. This is probably the reason why today's leaders fail in their duties. If only leaders' main concern were individuals, the last ones would be surrounded by a positive atmosphere of security, acknowledgement and respect. After all, leaders are expected to inspire trust to their people. The best possible environment is one that provides clear directions, cordial support and specific values. As Thucydides neatly put it, the town is mainly the people that reside in it, rather than its walls or navy.

'People matter'; this is a motto you are most likely to frequently hear from fake leaders, whose sole purpose is an increase in their profits out of a given company/organisation, or out of given authorities. In stead of embracing that kind of attitude, it is rather advisable to invest in your people in order to attain the figures you desire.

Change your attitude towards your people. Money is not an end in itself. Instead, enthusiasm and faith in a common goal or vision are most likely to prove of benefit. Do not forget that people are expecting a favourable attitude on your part in order to be able to perform more effectively. Give them a sense of purpose and a sense of belonging. Finally, stay true to them. Quite a few leaders seem to have forgotten the essential parameters of change and have thus failed to focus where it matters.

Leaders go for the heart before asking for a helping hand. This must be your final conclusion since at this point the book is coming to an end.

Reasons for this working attempt vary. It may be of importance to some and of none importance to others. For these first ones, it might be a cry for something different. A force towards change, may this be at a level of a society, of an organisation or at an individual level. Even more, it might be source of motivation for relative action; a force we all posses deep inside and has to be awakened. It is possible!

This book may also be the rise of a wave of creation, by means of changing certain things and destroying others. A drive to set the mind into motion. To do something . . .

As some familiar strangers might suspect . . . the journey now comes to an end.

Conclusion

It is commonly acceptable that nowadays, social policies and various forms of state intervention of a social character have been rendered of secondary importance. The socioeconomic state of European countries calls for a new form of leadership: one which will be likely to give rise to development and progress. This is not necessarily a hint for the new government; the last one might as well fail. It is about a new kind of leader who will drive individuals and organisations to a dignified place. It is to be questioned whether the word *abundance* is still part of our vocabulary. Nevertheless, through the progress out of proper allocation and management of available resources, it might as well regain its initial meaning.

News projected by mass media, senseless governments and often leaderships of organisations, as well as bureaucracy and its derived stiffness and financial irresolution in every part of human activity are only a few of the features of today's reality. The new leader/hero must face all of the above circumstances and treat them effectively. It is unknown whether success will finally come. Whether we are gradually moving towards new forms of leadership by individuals who are determined to manage our society in the way they have managed their organisations, is a question yet to be answered. The definite thing is that leaders of today's political system have failed. Indeed, this does not imply that successful managers or individuals who effectively resolve unfortunate issues are heroes; neither does it mean that successful organisations/businesses should be compared to political governments, since management of a country is far more complex than the management of an organisation. In no case is a paragon between the two intended.

In final analysis, the leaders of tomorrow resemble some sort of heroes who are expected to effectively overcome obstacles rising in the way of progress. It is difficult to imagine the way societies will look like in 10-15 years from now or which models will be adopted by given organisation leaders/administration. Yet, one thing is for sure. New models spring from different backgrounds (political leadership, sports, art) and what is likely to prevail in the end is what makes people happy and devoid of survival stress. Is such possible? This remains unknown. Is it unrealistic? Probably. Possibly too oriented to principles of Christianity? Maybe. In any case, it will definitely be better than what we are currently going through.

This book involves certain marketing, management and psychology concepts, notions and theories, aiming to help the reader shape a broader impression of external reality. It is an attempt to motivate people on a collective or individual basis and render them competitive in such a manner as to constitute a model figure for the rest of the society. The combination of such theories aims at rendering the reader more aware of current circumstances, in order to trigger considerations of change, may this be social, personal or professional.

One might wonder about the association between different concepts included in thus work, some of which are perception, creativity, benchmarking and personal improvement. Questions raised in the book, as well as various suggestions, serve to stimulate contemplation on such issues and motivate the reader to change. Change should be seen as an opportunity for improvement, or for shaping such circumstances as to allow for treatment of undesirable situations and attitudes.

Moreover, the book includes some steps to be followed in order for the reader to enhance certain 'established' attitudes most of the people adopt towards certain things.

How do creativity and inspiration work?
How can we stimulate them?
Which are the functions of human conscience and what do they serve for?
Which features of our thought processes are positive and which of them are negative?
Which of them require more attention and which require improvement?
What makes people change?
What can individuals do in order to attain personal and professional success?
How do people become leaders?

The above are only some of the questions raised in the book. An attempt is made to provide a plausible answer, in order to render the reader more aware of such concerns and stimulate a change for the better; for something different.

Bibliography— Sources—Ideas

Edgar Schein, (2004), *Organizational Culture and Leadership*, John Wiley & Sons

Chiotis, P. (1998) *Η παράδοση του Διαφωτισμού στην Ελλάδα (Tradition of Enlightenment in Greece)*. Athens: Enalios Publishers.

Collins, J. (2001). *From Good to Great*. New York: Random House.

De Bono, E. (1971). *The Use of Lateral Thinking*. London: Penguin.

Gross, R. (2002). *Socrates' Way: Seven Master Keys to Using Your Mind to the Utmost*. New York: Tarcher/Putnam.

Harris, T. (1969). *I'm OK/You're OK: A Practical Guide to Transactional Analysis*. New York: Harper and Row.

Institute, T. A. (2002). *Leadership and Self-deception: Getting Out of the Box*. San Francisco, CA: Berrett-Koehler.

Kioustelidis, I. (2002). *Ο Μηχανισμός της Νόησης (The Mechanism of Intellect)*. Athens: Papasotiriou Publications.

Mavroudis, G. (2004). *Η Τέχνη της ηγεσίας (The Art of Leadership)* Athens: Leader Books.

Miller, A. (2001). *Einstein, Picasso: Space, Time, and the Beauty That Causes Havoc*. New York: Basic Books.

Mulgan, G. (1997). *Connexity*. London: Jonathon Cape.

Peck, S. (1978). *The Road Less Traveled: A New Psychology of Love, Traditional Values and Spiritual Growth*. New York: Simon & Schuster.

Sandhusen, L. Richard (1993). *Markenting*. Barron's Educational Series.

Tjosvold, D. &. Tjosvold, Mary, M. (1995). *Psychology for Leaders*. New York: John Wiley & Sons Press.